HATS

by

Julia Holt,
Jane Mann
&
Karen Beggs

Illustrations by Nell Sully
Cover by Nell Sully

Adult Literacy & Basic Skills Unit

NEWMAT

The Berridge Centre, Clarendon College, Nottingham.

Produced by NEWMAT — A Special Development Project
for Nottinghamshire County Council, funded by ALBSU.

Production by Peter Beynon.

British Library Cataloguing in Publication Data

Holt, Julia, *1954-*
   Hats.
   1. English language — Readers
   I. Title II. Mann, Jane, *1956-*
   III. National Institute of Adult Education (England and Wales),
   Adult Literacy and Basic Skills Unit
   428.6

   ISBN 1-871174-16-3

Typeset and printed by
The Russell Press, Gamble Street,
Nottingham NG7 4ET

First published 1989

Contents

Writing Credits

Julia Holt
The Housewife Plant

Grace

Wanted

The Other Side of the World

Jane Mann
Newsflash — Woman Seen Wearing Four Hats

Coping with the Common Cold

My Best Friend

Anna

The Walk Home

Karen Beggs
Dear Ann

Freedom

Thank you to all
the students and tutors
who helped with this book.

NEWSFLASH —
Woman Seen Wearing Four Hats

A woman was seen
in the High Street today
wearing four hats —
all at the same time!

She said to our reporter:
"It was easy when I was small.
I only had to wear one hat at a time.
But these days
as soon as I take one off
I have to put another one on.

"I have a different hat
for everyone's needs.
Sometimes I have to wear them all at once.

"Right now I've got four on —
Mother, Teacher, Nurse and Housewife.
I've got my *'Daughter Hat'* in my pocket
for when I go to see my mum.

"When the kids have gone to bed
I'll put on my *'Friend Hat'*
and ring up Meg.

"Perhaps I'll put on my *'Lover Hat'* later.

"When my Karen has her baby
I'll get a *'Grandmother Hat'*.

"I'm not the only one
to wear so many hats.
Just look," she said,
pointing to the other women in the High Street.

Coping with the Common Cold

You will need:

1 sick man

2 aspirin

1 hot lemon drink

Honey — 2 spoonfuls

Gin — as much as you like

Patience — as much as you can find

A smile — add when needed

What to do:

1. Bite your tongue —
   and don't ask why men get flu
   and women get colds.
2. Smile.

3. Give him two aspirin and tell him to go to bed.
4. Help him upstairs into the bedroom.
5. Open the window a bit
   so he gets some fresh air.

6. If he hasn't got any pyjamas
   offer him one of your nighties.
7. Tuck him in.
8. Make sure he's got plenty of Kleenex.
9. Ask him if he'd like a hot drink.
10. Be patient! Don't snap at him when he says
    "I don't know," in a sad little voice.
11. Smile.

12. Stamp downstairs to the kitchen.
13. Put water in the kettle and switch it on.
14. When the water's boiled,
    make a drink with lemon and honey.
15. Add a little cold water and stir well.

16. Take the drink up to him.
17. Smile.
18. Tell him he'll soon be better.
    The aspirin is working and the drink helps.
    He goes to sleep.
19. Go downstairs.

20. Get a glass and pour yourself a gin.
    Add ice or tonic if you like.
21. Sit down and put your feet up.
22. Now you can watch the TV
    or stroke the cat.
23. Enjoy your rest.
24. Smile.

My Best Friend

Rose: What would I do without you?
       When we were at school
       and Mr White made me cry,
       you stood up for me.

May: Well, what are friends for?
       When we were at school
       and I didn't eat my cabbage,
       they kept me in.
       You stood up for me.

Rose: What would I do without you?
       When we were girls
       and you got stuck in a tree,
       I didn't help.
       I just laughed and laughed.
       You didn't mind.

May: Well, what are friends for?
       When we were girls
       and you fell in the lake
       wearing my best skirt,
       I shouted at you.
       You didn't mind.

Rose: What would I do without you?
When I fell out with Frank
I thought the world was ending.
You helped me carry on.

May: Well, what are friends for?
When Jo left me
I thought my heart was broken.
You helped me carry on.

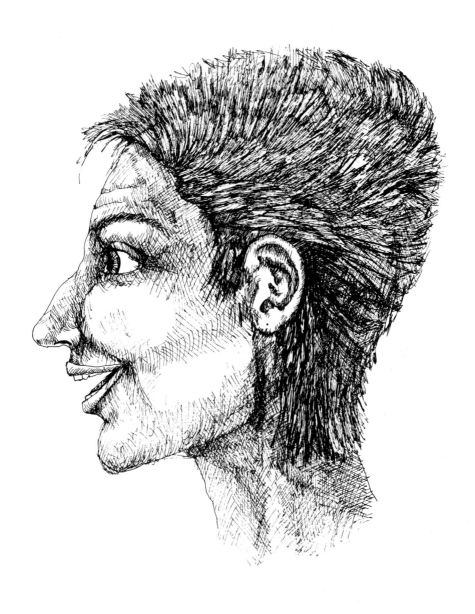

Rose: What would I do without you?
When my first baby was teething,
I didn't sleep at night
for months.
You kept me going.

May: Well, what are friends for?
When I thought I was pregnant
and I didn't want to be,
you talked to me.
You kept me going.

Rose: What would I do without you?
When Mum was ill and Jack lost his job,
I never thought I'd cope.
You were always there
when I needed you.

May: Well, what are friends for?
When Pat went to hospital,
I didn't know what to do.
You were always there
when I needed you.

Rose: All these years we've been friends.

May: All the good times and the bad times.

Rose: Our first bras.

May: Our first boyfriends.

Rose: Worrying about being fat.

May: Worrying about being thin.

Rose: Worrying about children.

May: Worrying about not having children.

Rose: Worrying about my job.

May: Worrying about not having a job.

Rose: School.

May: College.

Rose: Husbands.

May: Lovers.

Rose: You are always there.

May: My best friend.

The Housewife Plant

I am a housewife plant,
living in a marriage pot.

I am fed and watered,
Should I be grateful?

I am clipped and trimmed,
but I wanted to stretch.

I am shown with pride,
but only when I blossom.

I am making seeds,
potted, just like me.

I am pressing against the pot,
my roots want to grow.

I want to break the pot,
I want to be out.

I want to flower for myself,
I want to be in the garden.

If I don't bloom.
I'll be thrown out.

If I grow thorns,
I'll hurt someone.

If I shrink,
the pot won't feel too small.

Grace

I've just had the biggest baby in the world!
At least that's what it feels like
and I've got stitches to prove it.

I used to think
"What's all the fuss about.
You just go on with your life until the baby comes,
then it fits in with you
and 'Bingo' you have a family."

They said to me,
"This is the best time of your life."
and "Don't you look well."
I felt like a balloon.
I forgot what my feet were like.
I ate so much jam I looked like a strawberry.

"Whose baby is this?" I said.
"It's mine,
don't tell me how much to eat,
how much to work,
how much to grow."

I lived in fear of my waters breaking
in the supermarket or on the bus.
I was lucky, I was at home —
bag packed and ready.
The ambulance came, I said, "That's it."

Nobody said,
"Don't go into labour with mascara on
or in a new nightie."
I came out of the delivery room
looking like a panda
that had been dragged through a hedge backwards.

Then everybody comes to visit.
There you are with flowers and cards.
But the visitors come to see the baby,
not you.

Then, 'the naming of the parts':-
"She's got her Dad's nose."
"She's got her Grandma's ears."
"She's got her Uncle's legs."
How do they know?

Why do they say "Shhh, the baby's sleeping,"
when hospitals are full of noise.
I couldn't sleep.
The baby did.
They said, "You won't feel the pain."
I did.

I've had the biggest baby in the world.
But —
I've also had the best baby in the world.
She is perfect.
She smiles at me.

She holds my finger.
She cries a bit,
but not too much.
She looks like me.
I love her.
Her name is Grace.

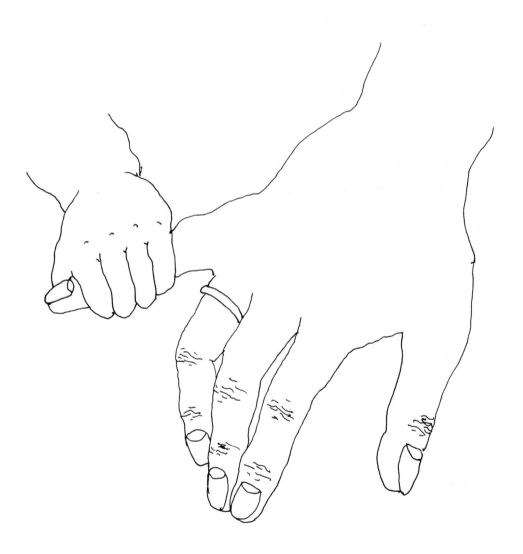

Anna

Ball. Yellow ball.
I want to play with my yellow ball.

I can't get it.
Mum keeps lifting me off the armchair.

I like the armchair.
It's soft for me to stroke.
Pretty for me to look at.
I can jump up and down on it.
Hide things down the back.
Here's my rusk. I put it there. I'll eat it.

There's my ball. I want it.
Mum's lifting me off again.
She doesn't understand.

I want the ball.
I want to ask for it, but I can't.
I know a few words.
But she doesn't understand them.

Can I say my name? What is it?
I think it's Anna, but Mum calls me Pet.
And Smelly Pants.
Gran calls me Flower.
I've got lots of names.

Here comes cat.
Come here cat, I want to hold you.
Let me hold your tail.
Soft fur, long black tail.
I'll pull it. **Ow!**

I want that ball.
"Ball, ball, ball, ball."
Why are they laughing at me?

What's that on the table?
I'll get on this chair and see.
Jam for me to put my hands in.
All red and sticky.
I'll tip it on the table.
It's all runny.
Put it in my mouth.
Mmm sweet.
I want to eat this **all** the time.

Mum looks cross.
Jam on the table. Jam on my dress.
Look there's the ball again.
It's on the armchair.
I can't get it.

I WANT IT NOW!

Wanted

Teacher Wanted —
for three children, ages five, seven and nine.

HOURS

6.00am to 9.00am

3.00pm to bedtime.

Every weekend and holidays.

On call 24 hours a day, 52 weeks a year.

QUALIFICATIONS

Must be able to answer these questions:-

a) Mum, why don't flies drown when it rains?

b) Mum, how many is none?

c) Mum, why can't I eat chips every day?

d) Mum, why do bubbles go pop?

e) Mum, why is the sky blue?

f) Mum, why does everybody get cross
   when I say why?

Must be able to:-

a) Skip, play football or cops and robbers.

b) Make a paper plane that really flies.

c) Pretend to be a robot, monster or horse.

d) Paint a picture of anything.

e) Mend bikes.

f) Make cabbage nice to eat.

The woman who gets this job will not lose her temper,
even in the supermarket.
She will do this work without training.
She will be able to think on her feet
and have an answer for every question.

PAY
Nothing.

OVERTIME
Everyday.

BONUS
Headaches.
An empty purse.
Lack of sleep.
No time for yourself.
Happy children.

APPLY
To our house —
PLEASE!

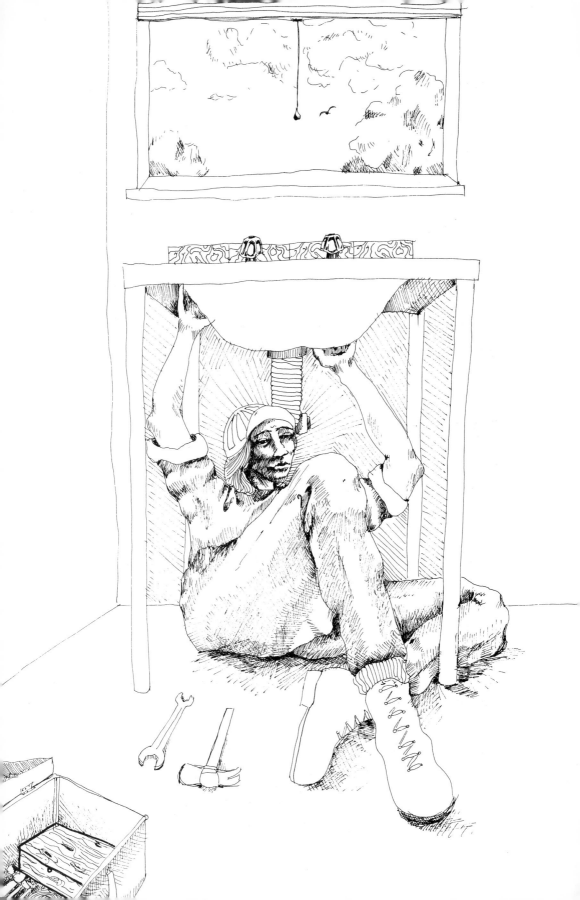

Dear Ann

17 Green Lane
West Hallam
Nottinghamshire

17 January 1989

Dear Ann,

Thank you for your letter. I am so proud of you. I never thought my daughter would become a plumber! And with the best marks in the class! What did the lads say?

I don't understand what the Women's Training Scheme is, but it sounds a great idea. It's time that women were given the chance to do jobs where they can stand on their own two feet and earn good money. I wish I could do it, but I think I'm too old to learn anything new.

Do you think you'll get a job? It's hard to find work these days and you've got to compete against the men.
You could start by coming to do some jobs for me.
Your Dad never gets anything finished!

Well Ann, I'll stop now. But remember we love you and we are very proud of you.

Lots of love, Mum xxxx

The Walk Home

It had been a good party
but for Trev.
Liz had a bit of a dance
and chatted with everybody.
The food and drink had been good too.

Trev had said,
"Cheer up love,"
when she didn't smile.
"I'll take you home."
She knew there was more to it
than just a lift,
so she said, "No thanks."
He was the kind
who didn't take no for an answer.

He said,
"Come on, don't be silly,
I won't rape you."
But she didn't know that.

So she still said "No."

She shut the door behind her
and turned her coat collar up.
The air felt sharp and cold
after the warm room at the party.

She shut the gate
and went up the empty street,
trying to look confident.
Perhaps if she looked confident
everybody would think she was.

She looked to see
which houses had lights on,
just in case.
She went down the main street,
trying not to run.
Trying not to hear the hooting cars
and the lads shouting.

She could get away from them
by going down the back streets.
But the back streets were dark
and the main street was well lit.
The back streets were a short cut.
She could be home sooner.
This didn't make her feel safer.
She left the main road
and went by the back streets.

She walked down the middle of the street
in case there was someone
behind the wall.
Anyway there was no traffic.

She kept seeing things
in the corner of her eye.
First a cat
then paper
blowing in the wind.

She was glad she was wearing jeans and flat shoes.
If she'd had money for a taxi
she could have put on her best dress.
Still, she knew she could run fast —
if she had to.
That's better than looking trendy.
Anyway her flat shoes were silent.
Not like the click clacking of high heels.

She turned into her street.
She felt in her pocket for the door keys.
Two more minutes
and she'd be home.

It was then that she saw him.
He was coming towards her.
Not a tall man
but a big man.
He had a firm step,
like hers.
But did he feel like her?

She felt sick
but didn't want to look it.
So she pulled herself up
to look big,
like cats do when dogs are close.

She didn't look at him,
in case he spoke.
She held on to her keys.
She could always hit him with them.

She went on
past her door.
He mustn't know
where her house was.

Ten steps past her door,
she looked back at the man.
Man?
It wasn't a man.
It was Cath from down the street.

"It's you,"
they both said at once.
"I could have sworn you were a man."

Cath said, "Do men feel like us
when they walk home in the dark?"

Liz was shivering.
"I wonder," she said.

The Other Side of the World

It seems like only yesterday
that I was six years old.
I remember playing in the sunshine.
Every day was sunny then.

I didn't think I would ever be this old.
Old in years may be
but not in my head.
I still feel six when the sun shines.

Little did I think
that at the far end of my life,
I would be at the other side of the world.

When I was six, my life was simple.
When I was thirty,
I had a small family to run.
Now I am sixty.
I am the head of a very big family.

Life is not simple any more.
My children, grandchildren and great grandchildren
all want me to help them.
They come to me and say —
"Shall we buy this house?"
"Shall I stay on at school?"
They always want to know what I think.

Life is full of changes.
Coming here was difficult
but I had to do the best for all of us.
Things change as you grow old.
Things change when you lose the ones you love.
Things change when you move home,
but coming to England
was the biggest change of all.

I sometimes think
that after a lifetime of hard work
it should be easy to please myself.
But this is the life I have.
I am not alone.

I think back
over all the things that I have done.
The ups and the downs.
The good times and the bad times.
But I wouldn't change a thing.

What is my secret?
How do I keep going?
I will tell you.
When things get bad,
I think about being six
and playing in the sunshine.

Freedom

It was 5 o'clock in the morning
and Helen didn't want to get out of bed.
It was just getting light outside.

"I hope it's a nice day," she thought.

She woke up her little girl, Trish.
They got dressed and had breakfast.

Then they went out into the yard
at the side of the house.
Two Volvo trucks were parked there.
A young man was sitting in one.

He leaned out of the window.
"Morning, Boss," he called to Helen.
"Lovely day."

"Morning, Mike," she replied.
"Let's go!"

Mike drove off.
Helen lifted Trish into the other truck
and climbed in after her.
They set off down the A46
to pick up the load.

It was almost 6 o'clock
when they pulled into the loading bay.
The foreman handed the delivery note to Helen.

He looked at her.
She wasn't more than 5 feet tall.
She was wearing jeans and a yellow T shirt,
with a yellow scarf in her hair.
She didn't look like a truck driver.

"You look well," he said.
"But I can't understand
why you want to do a man's job."

"Rubbish!" said Helen.
"I drive a truck because it pays.
I like the job and I do it well.
I've just got my second truck
and a man to work for me.
I can take Trish with me,
so I don't have to leave her
with a child-minder.
Anyway, I would hate a 9 to 5 job.
This job gives me freedom."

"Well, you're doing alright," he said.
"Good luck!"

Helen checked the load.
She swung the truck out of the yard
and headed for the M42.

The sun was shining.
She felt glad to be alive.
But most of all, she thought,
"I feel free!"

Other NEWMAT Titles

'Rock Biographies'

Twelve titles about key figures in rock music.

David Bowie	Elvis Presley
Bob Dylan	The Rolling Stones
John Lennon	Diana Ross
Madonna	The Sex Pistols
Bob Marley	Tina Turner
The Police	U2

'Routeing Around Wales'
'Routeing Around The Heart of England'

Two guide books to the sights, history and industry of places in the U.K. Illustrated with photographs, maps and diagrams.

'A Stab in the Heart'

A murder mystery story set in Los Angeles in 1940.

'Dogs and Roses'

A modern love story.
Illustrated with photographs.

Full details of these and forthcoming titles from:
ADULT LITERACY AND BASIC SKILLS UNIT
Kingsbourne House
229-231 High Holborn
London WC1V 7DA
Telephone: 01-405 4017

Telephone Number changes to:
071-405 4017 from 6th May 1990